NIBSY

AS

SANTA CLAUS

JACOB AUGUST RIIS

[ZHINGOORA BOOKS]

This edition is published by
Zhingoora Books.

The Cover is Designed by Pallav Sethiya.

CONTENTS

NIBSY'S CHRISTMAS

It was Christmas-eve over on the East Side. Darkness was closing in on a cold, hard day. The light that struggled through the frozen windows of the delicatessen store, and the saloon on the corner, fell upon men with empty dinner-pails who were hurrying homeward, their coats buttoned tightly, and heads bent against the steady blast from the river, as if they were butting their way down the street.

The wind had forced the door of the saloon ajar, and was whistling through the crack; but in there it seemed to make no one afraid. Between roars of laughter, the clink of glasses and the rattle of dice on the hard-wood counter were heard out in the street. More than one of the passers-by who came within range was taken with an extra shiver in which the vision of wife and little ones waiting at home for his coming was snuffed out, as he dropped in to brace up. The lights were long out when the silent streets re-echoed his unsteady steps toward home, where the Christmas welcome had turned to dread.

But in this twilight hour they burned brightly yet, trying hard to pierce the bitter cold outside with a ray of warmth and cheer. Where the lamps in the delicatessen store made a mottled streak of brightness across the flags, two little boys stood with their noses flattened against the window. Their warm breath made little round holes on the frosty pane, that came and went, affording passing glimpses of the wealth within, of the piles of smoked herring, of golden cheese, of sliced bacon and generous, fat-bellied hams; of the rows of odd-shaped bottles and jars on the shelves that

4

held there was no telling what good things, only it was certain that they must be good from the looks of them.

And the heavenly smell of spices and things that reached the boys through the open door each time the tinkling bell announced the coming or going of a customer! Better than all, back there on the top shelf the stacks of square honey-cakes, with their frosty coats of sugar, tied in bundles with strips of blue paper.

The wind blew straight through the patched and threadbare jackets of the lads as they crept closer to the window, struggling hard with the frost to make their peep-holes bigger, to take in the whole of the big cake with the almonds set in; but they did not heed it.

"Jim!" piped the smaller of the two, after a longer stare than usual; "hey, Jim! them's Sante Clause's. See 'em?"

"Sante Claus!" snorted the other, scornfully, applying his eye to the clear spot on the pane. "There ain't no ole duffer like dat. Them's honey-cakes. Me 'n' Tom had a bite o' one wunst."

"There ain't no Sante Claus?" retorted the smaller shaver, hotly, at his peep-hole. "There is, too. I seen him myself when he cum to our alley last——"

"What's youse kids a-scrappin' fur?" broke in a strange voice.

Another boy, bigger, but dirtier and tougher looking than either of the two, had come up behind them unobserved. He carried an armful of unsold "extras" under one arm. The other was buried to the elbow in the pocket of his ragged trousers.

The "kids" knew him, evidently, and the smallest eagerly accepted him as umpire.

"It's Jim w'at says there ain't no Sante Claus, and I seen him——"

"Jim!" demanded the elder ragamuffin, sternly, looking hard at the culprit; "Jim! y'ere a chump! No Sante Claus? What're ye givin' us? Now, watch me!"

With utter amazement the boys saw him disappear through the door under the tinkling bell into the charmed precincts of smoked herring, jam, and honey-cakes. Petrified at their peep-holes, they watched him, in the veritable presence of Santa Claus himself with the fir-branch, fish out five battered pennies from the depths of his pocket and pass them over to the woman behind the jars, in exchange for one of the bundles of honey-cakes tied with blue. As if in a dream they saw him issue forth with the coveted prize.

"There, kid!" he said, holding out the two fattest and whitest cakes to Santa Claus's champion; "there's yer Christmas. Run along, now, to yer barracks; and you, Jim, here's one for you, though yer don't desarve it. Mind ye let the kid alone."

"This one'll have to do for me grub, I guess. I ain't sold me 'Newses,' and the ole man'll kick if I bring 'em home."

And before the shuffling feet of the ragamuffins hurrying homeward had turned the corner, the last mouthful of the newsboy's supper was smothered in a yell of "Extree!" as he shot across the street to intercept a passing stranger.

As the evening wore on it grew rawer and more blustering still. Flakes of dry snow that stayed where they fell, slowly tracing the curb-lines, the shutters, and the doorsteps of the tenements with gathering white, were borne up on the storm from the water. To the right and left stretched endless streets between the towering barracks, as beneath frowning cliffs pierced with a thousand glowing eyes that revealed the watch-fires within—a mighty city of cave-dwellers held in the thraldom of poverty and want.

Outside there was yet hurrying to and fro. Saloon doors were slamming and bare-legged urchins, carrying beer-jugs, hugged the walls close for shelter. From the depths of a blind alley floated out the discordant strains of a vagabond brass band "blowing in" the yule of the poor. Banished by police ordinance from the street, it reaped a scant harvest of pennies for Christmas-cheer from the windows opening on the backyard. Against more than one pane showed the bald outline of a forlorn little Christmas-tree, some stray branch of a hemlock picked up at the grocer's and set in a pail for "the childer" to dance around, a dime's worth of candy and tinsel on the boughs.

From the attic over the way came, in spells between, the gentle tones of a German song about the Christ-child. Christmas in the East-Side tenements begins with the sunset on the "holy eve," except where the name is as a threat or a taunt. In a hundred such homes the whir of many sewing-machines, worked by the sweater's slaves with weary feet and aching backs, drowned every feeble note of joy that struggled to make itself heard above the noise of the great treadmill.

To these what was Christmas but the name for persecution, for suffering, reminder of lost kindred and liberty, of the slavery of eighteen hundred years, freedom from which was purchased only with gold. Aye, gold! The gold that had power to buy freedom yet, to buy the good will, aye, and the good name, of the oppressor, with his houses and land. At the thought the tired eye glistened, the aching back straightened, and to the weary foot there came new strength to finish the long task while the city slept.

Where a narrow passage-way put in between two big tenements to a ramshackle rear barrack, Nibsy, the newsboy, halted in the shadow of the doorway and stole a long look down the dark alley.

He toyed uncertainly with his still unsold papers—worn dirty and ragged as his clothes by this time—before he ventured in, picking his way between barrels and heaps of garbage; past the Italian cobbler's hovel, where a tallow dip, stuck in a cracked beer-glass, before a cheap print of the "Mother of God," showed that even he knew it was Christmas and liked to show it; past the Sullivan flat, where blows and drunken curses mingled with the shriek of women, as Nibsy had heard many nights before this one.

He shuddered as he felt his way past the door, partly with a premonition of what was in store for himself, if the "old man" was at home, partly with a vague, uncomfortable feeling that somehow Christmas-eve should be different from other nights, even in the alley. Down to its farthest end, to the last rickety flight of steps that led into the filth and darkness of the tenement. Up this he crept, three flights, to a door at which he stopped and listened, hesitating, as he had stopped at the entrance to the alley; then, with a sudden, defiant gesture, he pushed it open and went in.

A bare and cheerless room; a pile of rags for a bed in the corner, another in the dark alcove, miscalled bedroom; under the window a broken cradle and an iron-bound chest, upon which sat a sad-eyed woman with hard lines in her face, peeling potatoes in a pan; in the middle of the room a rusty stove, with a pile of wood, chopped on the floor alongside. A man on his knees in front fanning the fire with an old slouch hat. With each breath of draught he stirred, the crazy old pipe belched forth torrents of smoke at every point. As Nibsy entered, the man desisted from his efforts and sat up glaring at him. A villainous ruffian's face, scowling with anger.

"Late ag'in!" he growled; "an' yer papers not sold. What did I tell yer, brat, if ye dared——"

"Tom! Tom!" broke in the wife, in a desperate attempt to soothe the ruffian's temper.

"The boy can't help it, an' it's Christmas-eve. For the love o'——"

"To thunder with yer rot and with yer brat!" shouted the man, mad with the fury of passion. "Let me at him!" and, reaching over, he seized a heavy knot of wood and flung it at the head of the boy.

Nibsy had remained just inside the door, edging slowly toward his mother, but with a watchful eye on the man at the stove. At the first movement of his hand toward the woodpile he sprang for the stairway with the agility of a cat, and just dodged the missile. It struck the door, as he slammed it behind him, with force enough to smash the panel.

Down the three flights in as many jumps Nibsy went, and through the alley, over barrels and barriers, never stopping once till he reached the street, and curses and shouts were left behind.

In his flight he had lost his unsold papers, and he felt ruefully in his pocket as he went down the street, pulling his rags about him as much from shame as to keep out the cold.

Four pennies were all he had left after his Christmas treat to the two little lads from the barracks; not enough for supper or for a bed; and it was getting colder all the time.

On the sidewalk in front of the notion store a belated Christmas party was in progress. The children from the tenements in the alley and across the way were having a game of blindman's-buff, groping blindly about in the crowd to catch each other. They hailed Nibsy with shouts of laughter, calling to him to join in.

"We're having Christmas!" they yelled.

Nibsy did not hear them. He was thinking, thinking, the while turning over his four pennies at the bottom of his pocket.

Thinking if Christmas was ever to come to him, and the children's Santa Claus to find his alley where the baby slept within reach of her father's cruel hand. As for him, he had never known anything but blows and curses. He could take care of himself. But his mother and the baby——. And then it came to him with shuddering cold that it was getting late, and that he must find a place to sleep.

He weighed in his mind the merits of two or three places where he was in the habit of hiding from the "cops" when the alley got to be too hot for him.

There was the hay-barge down by the dock, with the watchman who got drunk sometimes, and so gave the boys a chance. The chances were at least even of its being available on Christmas-eve, and of Santa Claus having thus done him a good turn after all.

Then there was the snug berth in the sandbox you could curl all up in. Nibsy thought with regret of its being, like the hay-barge, so far away and to windward too.

Down by the printing-offices there were the steam-gratings, and a chance corner in the cellars, stories and stories underground, where the big presses keep up such a clatter from midnight till far into the day.

As he passed them in review, Nibsy made up his mind with sudden determination, and, setting his face toward the south, made off down town.

The rumble of the last departing news-wagon over the pavement, now buried deep in snow, had died away in the distance, when, from out of the bowels of the earth there issued a cry, a cry of mortal terror and pain that was echoed by a hundred throats.

From one of the deep cellar-ways a man ran out, his clothes and hair and beard afire; on his heels a breathless throng of men and boys; following them, close behind, a rush of smoke and fire.

The clatter of the presses ceased suddenly, to be followed quickly by the clangor of hurrying fire-bells. With hook and axes the firemen rushed in; hose was let down through the manholes, and down there in the depths the battle was fought and won.

The building was saved; but in the midst of the rejoicing over the victory there fell a sudden silence. From the cellar-way a grimy, helmeted figure arose, with something black and scorched in his arms. A tarpaulin was spread upon the snow and upon it he laid his burden, while the silent crowd made room and word went over to the hospital for the doctor to come quickly.

Very gently they lifted poor little Nibsy—for it was he, caught in his berth by a worse enemy than the "cop" or the watchman of the hay-barge—into the ambulance that bore him off to the hospital cot, too late.

Conscious only of a vague discomfort that had succeeded terror and pain, Nibsy wondered uneasily why they were all so kind. Nobody had taken the trouble to as much as notice him before. When he had thrust his papers into their very faces they had pushed him roughly aside. Nibsy, unhurt and able to fight his way, never had a show. Sick and maimed and sore, he was being made much of, though he had been caught where the boys were forbidden to go. Things were queer, anyhow, and——

The room was getting so dark that he could hardly see the doctor's kindly face, and had to grip his hand tightly to make sure that he was there; almost as dark as the stairs in the alley he had come down in such a hurry.

There was the baby now—poor baby—and mother—and then a great blank, and it was all a mystery to poor Nibsy no longer. For, just as a wild-eyed woman pushed her way through the crowd of nurses and doctors to his bedside, crying for her boy, Nibsy gave up his soul to God.

It was very quiet in the alley. Christmas had come and gone. Upon the last door a bow of soiled crape was nailed up with two tacks. It had done duty there a dozen times before, that year.

Upstairs, Nibsy was at home, and for once the neighbors, one and all, old and young, came to see him.

Even the father, ruffian that he was, offered no objection. Cowed and silent, he sat in the corner by the window farthest from where the plain little coffin stood, with the lid closed down.

A couple of the neighbor-women were talking in low tones by the stove, when there came a timid knock at the door. Nobody answering, it was pushed open, first a little, then far enough to admit the shrinking form of a little ragamuffin, the smaller of the two who had stood breathing peep-holes on the window-pane of the delicatessen store the night before when Nibsy came along.

He dragged with him a hemlock branch, the leavings from some Christmas-tree fitted into its block by the grocer for a customer.

"It's from Sante Claus," he said, laying it on the coffin. "Nibsy knows." And he went out.

Santa Claus had come to Nibsy, after all, in his alley. And Nibsy knew.

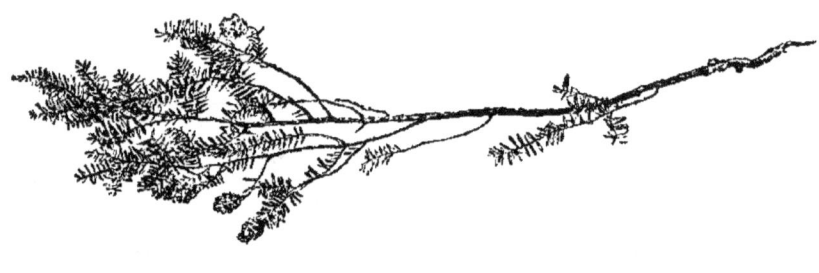

WHAT THE CHRISTMAS SUN SAW IN THE TENEMENTS

The December sun shone clear and cold upon the city. It shone upon rich and poor alike. It shone into the homes of the wealthy on the avenues and in the uptown streets, and into courts and alleys hedged in by towering tenements down town. It shone upon throngs of busy holiday shoppers that went out and in at the big stores, carrying bundles big and small, all alike filled with Christmas cheer and kindly messages from Santa Claus.

It shone down so gayly and altogether cheerily there, that wraps and overcoats were unbuttoned for the north wind to toy with. "My, isn't it a nice day?" said one young lady in a fur shoulder-cape to a friend, pausing to kiss and compare lists of Christmas gifts.

"Most too hot," was the reply, and the friends passed on. There was warmth within and without. Life was very pleasant under the Christmas sun up on the avenue.

Down in Cherry Street the rays of the sun climbed over a row of tall tenements with an effort that seemed to exhaust all the life that was in them, and fell into a dirty block, half-choked with trucks, with ash-barrels and rubbish of all sorts, among which the dust was whirled in clouds upon fitful, shivering blasts that searched every nook and cranny of the big barracks. They fell upon a little girl, bare-footed and in rags, who struggled out of an alley with a broken pitcher in her grimy fist, against the wind that set down the narrow slit like the draught through a big factory chimney. Just at the mouth of the alley it took her with a sudden whirl, a cyclone of dust and drifting ashes, tossed her fairly off her feet, tore from her grip the threadbare shawl she clutched at her throat, and set her down at the saloon-door breathless and half-smothered. She had just time to dodge through the storm-doors before another whirlwind swept whistling down the street.

"My, but isn't it cold?" she said, as she shook the dust out of her shawl and set the pitcher down on the bar. "Gimme a pint," laying down a few pennies that had been wrapped in a corner of the shawl, "and mamma says make it good and full."

"All'us the way with youse kids—want a barrel when yees pays fer a pint," growled the bartender. "There, run along, and don't ye hang around that stove no more. We ain't a steam-heatin' the block fer nothin'."

The little girl clutched her shawl and the pitcher, and slipped out into the street where the wind lay in ambush and promptly bore down on her in pillars of whirling dust as soon as she appeared. But the sun that pitied her bare feet and little frozen hands played a trick on old Boreas—it showed her a way between the pillars, and only just her skirt was caught by one and whirled over her head as she dodged into her alley. It peeped after her half-way down its dark depths, where it seemed colder even than in the bleak street, but there it had to leave her.

It did not see her dive through the doorless opening into a hall where no sun-ray had ever entered. It could not have found its way in there had it tried. But up the narrow, squeaking stairs the girl with the pitcher was climbing. Up one flight of stairs, over a knot of children, half babies, pitching pennies on the landing, over wash-tubs and bedsteads that encumbered the next—house-cleaning going on in that "flat;" that is to say, the surplus of bugs was being burned out with petroleum and a feather—up still another, past a half-open door through which came the noise of brawling and curses. She dodged and quickened her step a little until she stood panting before a door on the fourth landing that opened readily as she pushed it with her bare foot.

A room almost devoid of stick or rag one might dignify with the name of furniture. Two chairs, one with a broken back, the other on three legs, beside a rickety table that stood upright only by leaning against the wall. On the unwashed floor a heap of straw covered with dirty bed-tick for a bed; a foul-smelling slop-pail in the middle of the room; a crazy stove, and back of it a door or gap opening upon darkness. There was something in there, but what it was could only be surmised from a heavy snore that rose and fell regularly. It was the bedroom of the apartment, windowless, airless, and sunless, but rented at a price a millionaire would denounce as robbery.

"That you, Liza?" said a voice that discovered a woman bending over the stove. "Run 'n' get the childer. Dinner's ready."

The winter sun glancing down the wall of the opposite tenement, with a hopeless effort to cheer the backyard, might have peeped through the one window of the room in Mrs. McGroarty's "flat," had that window not been coated with the dust of ages, and discovered that dinner-party in action. It might have found a hundred like it in the alley. Four unkempt children, copies each in his or her way of Liza and their mother, Mrs. McGroarty, who "did washing" for a living. A meat bone, a "cut" from the butcher's at four cents a pound, green pickles, stale bread and beer. Beer for the four, a sup all round, the baby included. Why not? It was the one relish the searching ray would have found there. Potatoes were there, too—potatoes and meat! Say not the poor in the tenements are starving. In New York only those starve who cannot get work and have not the courage to beg. Fifty thousand always out of a job, say those who pretend to know. A round half-million asking and getting charity in eight years, say the statisticians of the Charity Organization. Any one can go round and see for himself that no one need starve in New York.

From across the yard the sunbeam, as it crept up the wall, fell slantingly through the attic window whence issued the sound of hammer-blows. A man with a hard face stood in its light, driving nails into the lid of a soap-box that was partly filled with straw. Something else was there; as he shifted the lid that didn't fit, the glimpse of sunshine fell across it; it was a dead child, a little baby in a white slip, bedded in straw in a soap-box for a coffin. The man was hammering down the lid to take it to the Potter's Field. At the bed knelt the mother, dry-eyed, delirious from starvation that had killed her child. Five hungry, frightened children cowered in the corner, hardly daring to whisper as they looked from the father to the mother in terror.

There was a knock on the door that was drowned once, twice, in the noise of the hammer on the little coffin. Then it was opened gently, and a young woman came in with a basket. A little silver cross shone upon her breast. She went to the poor mother, and putting her hand soothingly on her head knelt by her with gentle and loving words. The half-crazed woman listened with averted face, then suddenly burst into tears and hid her throbbing head in the other's lap.

The man stopped hammering and stared fixedly upon the two; the children gathered around with devouring looks as the visitor took from her basket bread, meat, and tea. Just then, with a parting, wistful look into the bare attic room, the sun-ray slipped away, lingered for a moment about the coping outside and fled over the house-tops.

As it sped on its winter-day journey, did it shine into any cabin in an Irish bog more desolate than these Cherry Street "homes?" An army of thousands whose one bright and wholesome memory, only tradition of home, is that poverty-stricken cabin in the desolate bog, are herded in such barracks to-day in New York. Potatoes they have; yes, and meat at four cents—even seven. Beer for a relish—never without beer. But home? The home that was home even in a bog, with the love of it that has made Ireland immortal and a tower of strength in the midst of her suffering— what of that? There are no homes in New York's poor tenements.

Down the crooked path of the Mulberry Street Bend the sunlight slanted into the heart of New York's Italy. It shone upon bandannas and yellow neckerchiefs; upon swarthy faces and corduroy breeches; upon blackhaired girls—mothers at thirteen; upon hosts of bow-legged children rolling in the dirt; upon pedlers' carts and ragpickers staggering under burdens that threatened to crush them at every step. Shone upon unnumbered Pasquales dwelling, working, idling, and gambling there. Shone upon the filthiest and foulest of New York's tenements, upon Bandits' Roost, upon Bottle Alley, upon the hidden by-ways that lead to the tramp's burrows. Shone upon the scene of annual infant slaughter. Shone into the foul core of New York's slums that is at last to go to the realm of bad memories because civilized man may not look upon it and live without blushing.

It glanced past the rag-shop in the cellar, whence welled up stenches to poison the town, into an apartment three flights up that held two women, one young, the other old and bent. The young one had a baby at her breast. She was rocking it tenderly in her arms, singing in the soft Italian tongue a lullaby, while the old granny listened eagerly, her elbows on her knees, and a stumpy clay-pipe, blackened with age, between her teeth. Her eyes were set on the wall, on which the musty paper hung in tatters, fit frame for the wretched, poverty-stricken room, but they saw neither poverty nor want; her aged limbs felt not the cold draught from without, in which they shivered; they looked far over the seas to sunny Italy, whose music was in her ears.

"O dolce Napoli," she mumbled between her toothless jaws, "O suol beato——"

The song ended in a burst of passionate grief. The old granny and the baby woke up at once. They were not in sunny Italy; not under Southern, cloudless skies. They were in "The Bend" in Mulberry Street, and the wintry wind rattled the door as if it would say, in the language of their new home, the land of the free: "Less music! More work! Root, hog, or die!"

Around the corner the sunbeam danced with the wind into Mott Street, lifted the blouse of a Chinaman and made it play tag with his pig-tail. It used him so roughly that he was glad to skip from it down a cellar-way that gave out fumes of opium strong enough to scare even the north wind from its purpose. The soles of his felt shoes showed as he disappeared down the ladder that passed for cellar-steps. Down there, where daylight never came, a group of yellow, almond-eyed men were bending over a table playing fan-tan. Their very souls were in the game, every faculty of the mind bent on the issue and the stake. The one blouse that was indifferent to what went on was stretched on a mat in a corner. One end of a clumsy pipe was in his mouth, the other held over a little spirit-lamp on the divan on which he lay. Something spluttered in the flame with a pungent, unpleasant smell. The smoker took a long draught, inhaling the white smoke, then sank back on his couch in senseless content.

Upstairs tiptoed the noiseless felt shoes, bent on some house errand, to the "household" floors above, where young white girls from the tenements of The Bend and the East Side live in slavery worse, if not more galling, than any of the galley with ball and chain—the slavery of the pipe. Four, eight, sixteen—twenty odd such "homes" in this tenement, disgracing the very name of home and family, for marriage and troth are not in the bargain.

In one room, between the half-drawn curtains of which the sunbeam works its way in, three girls are lying on as many bunks, smoking all. They are very young, "under age," though each and every one would glibly swear in court to the satisfaction of the police that she is sixteen, and therefore free to make her own bad choice. Of these, one was brought up among the rugged hills of Maine; the other two are from the tenement crowds, hardly missed there. But their companion? She is twirling the sticky brown pill over the lamp, preparing to fill the bowl of her pipe with it. As she does so, the sunbeam dances across the bed, kisses the red spot on her cheek that betrays the secret her tyrant long has known, though to her it is hidden yet—that the pipe has claimed its victim and soon will pass it on to the Potter's Field.

"Nell," says one of her chums in the other bunk, something stirred within her by the flash—"Nell, did you hear from the old farm to home since you come here?"

Nell turns half around, with the toasting-stick in her hand, an ugly look on her wasted features, a vile oath on her lips.

"To hell with the old farm," she says, and putting the pipe to her mouth inhales it all, every bit, in one long breath, then falls back on her pillow in drunken stupor.

That is what the sun of a winter day saw and heard in Mott Street.

It had travelled far toward the west, searching many dark corners and vainly seeking entry to others; had gilt with equal impartiality the spires of five hundred churches and the tin cornices of thirty thousand tenements, with their million tenants and more; had smiled courage and cheer to patient mothers trying to make the most of life in the teeming crowds, that had too little sunshine by far; hope to toiling fathers striving early and late for bread to fill the many mouths clamoring to be fed.

The brief December day was far spent. Now its rays fell across the North River and lighted up the windows of the tenements in Hell's Kitchen and Poverty Gap. In the Gap especially they made a brave show; the windows of the crazy old frame-house under the big tree that set back from the street looked as if they were made of beaten gold. But the glory did not cross the threshold. Within it was dark and dreary and cold. The room at the foot of the rickety, patched stairs was empty. The last tenant was beaten to death by her husband in his drunken fury. The sun's rays shunned the spot ever after, though it was long since it could have made out the red daub from the mould on the rotten floor.

Upstairs, in the cold attic, where the wind wailed mournfully through every open crack, a little girl sat sobbing as if her heart would break. She hugged an old doll to her breast. The paint was gone from its face; the yellow hair was in a tangle; its clothes hung in rags. But she only hugged it closer. It was her doll. They had been friends so long, shared hunger and hardship together, and now——.

Her tears fell faster. One drop trembled upon the wan cheek of the doll. The last sunbeam shot athwart it and made it glisten like a priceless jewel. Its glory grew and filled the room. Gone were the black walls, the darkness and the cold. There was warmth and light and joy. Merry voices and glad faces were all about. A flock of children danced with gleeful shouts about a great Christmas-tree in the middle of the floor. Upon its branches hung drums and trumpets and toys, and countless candles gleamed like beautiful stars. Farthest up, at the very top, her doll, her very own, with arms outstretched, as if appealing to be taken down and hugged. She knew it, knew the mission-school that had seen her first and only real Christmas, knew the gentle face of her teacher, and the writing on the wall she had taught her to spell out: "In His Name." His name, who, she had said, was all little children's friend. Was he also her dolly's friend, and would know it among the strange people?

The light went out; the glory faded. The bare room, only colder and more cheerless than before, was left. The child shivered. Only that morning the doctor had told her mother that she must have medicine and food and warmth, or she must go to the great hospital where papa had gone before, when their money was all spent. Sorrow and want had laid the mother upon the bed he had barely left. Every stick of furniture, every stitch of clothing on which money could be borrowed, had gone to the pawnbroker. Last of all, she had carried mamma's wedding-ring, to pay the druggist. Now there was no more left, and they had nothing to eat. In a little while mamma would wake up, hungry.

The little girl smothered a last sob and rose quickly. She wrapped the doll in a threadbare shawl, as well as she could, tiptoed to the door and listened a moment to the feeble breathing of the sick mother within. Then she went out, shutting the door softly behind her, lest she wake her.

Up the street she went, the way she knew so well, one block and a turn round the saloon corner, the sunset glow kissing the track of her bare feet in the snow as she went, to a door that rang a noisy bell as she opened it and went in. A musty smell filled the close room. Packages, great and small, lay piled high on shelves behind the worn counter. A slovenly woman was haggling with the pawnbroker about the money for a skirt she had brought to pledge.

"Not a cent more than a quarter," he said, contemptuously, tossing the garment aside. "It's half worn out it is, dragging it back and forth over the counter these six months. Take it or leave it. Hallo! What have we here? Little Finnegan, eh? Your mother not dead yet? It's in the poor-house ye will be if she lasts much longer. What the——"

He had taken the package from the trembling child's hand—the precious doll—and unrolled the shawl. A moment he stood staring in dumb amazement at its contents. Then he caught it up and flung it with an angry oath upon the floor, where it was shivered against the coal-box.

"Get out o' here, ye Finnegan brat," he shouted; "I'll tache ye to come a'guyin' o' me. I'll——"

The door closed with a bang upon the frightened child, alone in the cold night. The sun saw not its home-coming. It had hidden behind the night-clouds, weary of the sight of man and his cruelty.

Evening had worn into night. The busy city slept. Down by the wharves, now deserted, a poor boy sat on the bulwark, hungry, footsore, and shivering with cold. He sat thinking of friends and home, thousands of miles away over the sea, whom he had left six months before to go among strangers. He had been alone ever since, but never more so than that night. His money gone, no work to be found, he had slept in the streets for nights. That day he had eaten nothing; he would rather die than beg, and one of the two he must do soon.

There was the dark river, rushing at his feet; the swirl of the unseen waters whispered to him of rest and peace he had not known since——it was so cold—and who was there to care, he thought bitterly. No one who would ever know. He moved a little nearer the edge, and listened more intently.

A low whine fell on his ear, and a cold, wet face was pressed against his. A little, crippled dog that had been crouching silently beside him nestled in his lap. He had picked it up in the street, as forlorn and friendless as himself, and it had stayed by him. Its touch recalled him to himself. He got up hastily, and, taking the dog in his arms, went to the police station near by and asked for shelter. It was the first time he had accepted even such charity, and as he lay down on his rough plank he hugged a little gold locket he wore around his neck, the last link with better days, and thought, with a hard, dry sob, of home.

In the middle of the night he awoke with a start. The locket was gone. One of the tramps who slept with him had stolen it. With bitter tears he went up and complained to the Sergeant at the desk, and the Sergeant ordered him to be kicked out in the street as a liar, if not a thief. How should a tramp boy have come honestly by a gold locket? The doorman put him out as he was bidden, and when the little dog showed its teeth, a policeman seized it and clubbed it to death on the step.

Far from the slumbering city the rising moon shines over a wide expanse of glistening water. It silvers the snow upon a barren heath between two shores, and shortens with each passing minute the shadows of countless headstones that bear no names, only numbers. The breakers that beat against the bluff wake not those who sleep there. In the deep trenches they lie, shoulder to shoulder, an army of brothers, homeless in life, but here at rest and at peace. A great cross stands upon the lonely shore. The moon sheds its rays upon it in silent benediction and floods the garden of the unknown, unmourned dead with its soft light. Out on the Sound the fishermen see it flashing white against the starlit sky, and bare their heads reverently as their boats speed by, borne upon the wings of the west wind.

SKIPPY OF SCRABBLE ALLEY

Skippy was at home in Scrabble Alley. So far as he had ever known home of any kind it was there in the dark and mouldy basement of the rear house, farthest back in the gap that was all the builder of those big tenements had been able to afford of light and of air for the poor people whose hard-earned wages, brought home every Saturday, left them as poor as if they had never earned a dollar, to pile themselves up in his strong-box. The good man had long since been gathered to his fathers—gone to his better home. It was in the newspapers, and in the alley it was said that it was the biggest funeral—more than a hundred carriages, and four black horses to pull the hearse. So it must be true, of course.

Skippy wondered vaguely, sometimes, when he thought of it, what kind of a home it might be where people went in a hundred carriages. He had never sat in one. The nearest he had come to it was when Jimmy Murphy's cab had nearly run him down once, and his "fare," a big man with whiskers, had put his head out and angrily called him a brat, and told him to get out of the way, or he would have him arrested. And Jimmy had shaken his whip at him and told him to skip home. Everybody told him to skip. From the policeman on the block to the hard-fisted man he knew as his father, and who always had a job for him with the growler when he came home, they were having Skippy on the run. Probably that was how he got his name. No one cared enough about it, or about the boy, to find out.

Was there anybody anywhere who cared about boys, anyhow? Were there any boys in that other home where the carriages and the big hearse had gone? And if there were, did they have to live in an alley, and did they ever have any fun? These were thoughts that puzzled Skippy's young brain once in a while. Not very long or very hard, for Skippy had not been trained to think; what training the boys picked up in the alley didn't run much to deep thinking.

Perhaps it was just as well. There were one or two men there who were said to know a heap, and who had thought and studied it all out about the landlord and the alley. But it was very tiresome that it should happen to be just those two, for Skippy never liked them. They were always cross and ugly, never laughed and carried on as the other men did once in a while, and made his little feet very tired running with the growler early and late. He well remembered, too, that it was one of them who had said, when they brought him home, sore and limping, from under the wheels of Jimmy Murphy's cab, that he'd been better off if it had killed him. He had always borne a grudge against him for that, for there was no occasion for it that he could see. Hadn't he been to the gin-mill for him that very day twice?

Skippy's horizon was bounded by the towering brick walls of Scrabble Alley. No sun ever rose or set between them. On the hot summer days, when the saloon-keeper on the farther side of the street pulled up his awning, the sun came over the house-tops and looked down for an hour or two into the alley. It shone upon broken flags, a mud-puddle by the hydrant where the children went splashing with dirty, bare feet, and upon unnumbered ash-barrels. A stray cabbage-leaf in one of these was the only green thing it found, for no ray ever strayed through the window in Skippy's basement to trace the green mould on the wall.

Once, while he had been lying sick with a fever, Skippy had struck up a real friendly acquaintance with that mouldy wall. He had pictured to himself woods and hills and a regular wilderness, such as he had heard of, in its green growth; but even that pleasure they had robbed him of. The charity doctor had said that the mould was bad, and a man scraped it off and put whitewash on the wall. As if everything that made fun for a boy was bad.

Down the street a little way was a yard just big enough and nice to play ball in, but the agent had put up a sign that he would have no boys and no ball-playing in his yard, and that ended it; for the "cop" would have none of it in the street either. Once he had caught them at it and "given them the collar." They had been up before the judge, and though he let them off they had been branded, Skippy and the rest, as a bad lot.

That was the starting-point in Skippy's career. With the brand upon him he accepted the future it marked out for him, reasoning as little, or as vaguely, about the justice of it as he had about the home conditions of the alley. The world, what he had seen of it, had taught him one lesson: to take things as he found them, because that was the way they were; and that being the easiest, and, on the whole, best suited to Skippy's general make-up, he fell naturally into the rôle assigned him. After that he worked the growler on his own hook most of the time. The "gang" he had joined found means of keeping it going that more than justified the brand the policeman had put upon it. It was seldom by honest work. What was the use? The world owed them a living, and it was their business to collect it as easily as they could. It was everybody's business to do that, as far as they could see, from the man who owned the alley, down.

They made the alley pan out in their own way. It had advantages the builder hadn't thought of, though he provided them. Full of secret ins and outs, runways and passages, not easily found, to the surrounding tenements, it offered chances to get away when one or more of the gang were "wanted" for robbing this store on the avenue, tapping that till, or raiding the grocer's stock, that were A No. 1. When some tipsy man had been waylaid and "stood up," it was an unequalled spot for dividing the plunder. It happened once or twice, as time went by, that a man was knocked on the head and robbed within the bailiwick of the now notorious Scrabble Alley gang, or that a drowned man floated ashore in the dock with his pockets turned inside out. On such occasions the police made an extra raid, and more or less of the gang were scooped in, but nothing ever came of it. Dead men tell no tales, and they were not more silent than the Scrabbles, if, indeed, these had anything to tell.

It came gradually to be an old story. Skippy and his associates were long since in the Rogues' Gallery, numbered and indexed as truly a bad lot now. They were no longer boys, but toughs. Most of them had "done time" up the river and come back more hardened than they went, full of new tricks always, which they were eager to show the boys to prove that they had not been idle while they were away. On the police returns they figured as "speculators," a term that sounded better than thief, and meant, as they understood it, much the same, viz., a man who made a living out of other people's labor. It was conceded in the slums, everywhere, that the Scrabble-Alley gang was a little the boldest that had for a long time defied the police. It had the call in the other gangs in all the blocks around, for it had the biggest fighters as well as the cleverest thieves of them all.

Then one holiday morning, when in a hundred churches the pæan went up, "On earth peace, good-will toward men," all New York rang with the story of a midnight murder committed by Skippy's gang. The saloon-keeper whose place they were sacking to get the "stuff" for keeping Christmas in their way had come upon them, and Skippy had shot him down while the others ran. A universal shout for vengeance went up from outraged Society.

It sounded the death-knell of the gang. It was scattered to the four winds, all except Skippy, who was tried for murder and hanged. The papers spoke of his phenomenal calmness under the gallows; said it was defiance. The priest who had been with him in his last hours said he was content to go to a better home. They were all wrong. Had the pictures that chased each other across Skippy's mind as the black cap was pulled over his face been visible to their eyes, they would have seen Scrabble Alley with its dripping hydrant, and the puddle in which the children splashed with dirty, bare feet; the dark basement room with its mouldy wall; the notice in the yard, "No ball-playing allowed here;" the policeman who stamped him as one of a bad lot, and the sullen man who thought it had been better for him, the time he was run over, if he had died. Skippy asked himself moodily if he was right after all, and if boys were ever to have any show. He died with the question unanswered.

They said that no such funeral ever went out of Scrabble Alley before. There was a real raid on the undertaker's where Skippy lay in state two whole days, and the wake was talked of for many a day as something wonderful. At the funeral services it was said that without a doubt Skippy had gone to a better home. His account was squared.

Skippy's story is not invented to be told here. In its main facts it is a plain account of a well-remembered drama of the slums, on which the curtain was rung down in the Tombs yard. There are Skippies without number growing up in those slums to-day, vaguely wondering why they were born into a world that does not want them; Scrabble Alleys to be found for the asking, all over this big city where the tenements abound, alleys in which generations of boys have lived and died—principally died, and thus done for themselves the best they could, according to the crusty philosopher of Skippy's set—with nothing more inspiring than a dead blank wall within reach of their windows all the days of their cheerless lives. Theirs is the account to be squared—by justice, not vengeance. Skippy is but an item on the wrong side of the ledger. The real reckoning of outraged society is not with him, but with Scrabble Alley.

The End